Set *on* Fire

AN UNFORGETTABLE
JOURNEY
THROUGH TRIAL
INTO TRUST

Set *on* Fire

Sandra Siemens, LISW

SET ON FIRE

The views and opinions expressed in this book are those of the author and do not necessarily reflect the official policy or position of Illumify Media Global.

Published by
Illumify Media Global
www.IllumifyMedia.com
"Write. Publish. Market. *SELL!*"

Library of Congress Control Number: 2020922932

Paperback ISBN: 978-1-947360-68-6
eBook ISBN: 978-1-947360-69-3

Typeset by Art Innovations (http://artinnovations.in/)
Cover design by Debbie Lewis

Printed in the United States of America

Dedication

For my family, which includes my daughter, Sara, my son, Nick, his wife, Amie, and their daughter, Haley. They have been with me on this journey since the first time I was rushed to the hospital. They have given me the courage to press on, the joy of laughter, the reassurance of their prayers, their time, and their love. They are my first responders, and I am eternally grateful.

I also dedicate these words to Jesus. I felt inspired to draw this image shortly after my diagnosis. Whenever I look at it, I am reminded of the faithfulness of His precious presence, even when circumstances seem dark.

Epigraph

The word *inflammation* is from the Latin word *inflammare*, which means "to set on fire." According to Dr. Andrew Luster of the Center for Immunology and Inflammatory Diseases at Harvard-affiliated Massachusetts General Hospital, inflammation is "a smoldering process that injures your tissues, joints, and blood vessels, and you often do not notice it until significant damage is done." Chronic inflammation creates the same kind of destruction—except now the flame persists.

Contents

Prologue: The Park   xiii

1.   Fire Starter   1
2.   Someone Is Crying   9
3.   Ablaze with the Presence of God   14
4.   Fire and Water   19
5.   The Fiery Trial   28
6.   Fire and Ice   37
7.   The Little Pitcher   45
8.   A Flicker of Hope   50
9.   Little Fires Everywhere   57
10. Field Work   61
11. Forged in the Furnace of Affliction   67
12. I Saw Love   72
13. The Underground Work of the Cave Must Be Done   75
14. The Watering Place   81
15. The Seeds of Hope   86
16. The Glorious Leaf of Hope   89
17. Christmas Fire   92
18. Fire on the Mountain   96
19. The Fire of Rebirth   105

Epilogue   108
About the Author   110

Prologue

THE PARK

February 2009

I always knew I was supposed to do something meaningful for God. I don't know how I knew, I just did. I was convinced when I founded my Christian Counseling Company in 2000; this venture was the "something meaningful" I was purposed to do.

I believed in a big God who had a purpose and destiny for all of his children to accomplish. I had gone back to college to get my master's degree in social work. The company was growing and expanding as staff and therapists worked with individuals, families, couples, and children. We were making a difference.

And then I got sick, and everything changed.

I struggled to resign myself to a small existence. I attempted to shrink my expectations. Despite that, I could not put out the passionate fire I felt inside to accomplish something for God. Inevitably, just when I had decided to let my fire die out, I would come across a rousing sermon or recharging scripture, and the spark would set my soul ablaze.

One wintry February afternoon in 2009, three years after receiving my devastating diagnosis, I drove to Duck Creek Park, in Davenport, Iowa. I was aware that something extraordinary was about to be revealed. The God of new things was summoning me to my destiny.

I could sense something was about to unfold. I was not sure what it was.

I had been to the park many times over the years. I especially enjoyed the park in the spring when rows and rows of rich, purple lilacs overflowed the entire park with their fragrant perfume. This afternoon, however, the park was a cold, desolate wilderness. Naked, sleeping trees and patches of dirty gray snow speckled the ground.

As the afternoon progressed, light snowflakes began to fall, along with tiny pellets of frozen rain. Visibility was soon going to become compromised.

As midafternoon turned to early evening, I was restless. Glancing at the clock on my instrument panel, I realized it was getting late. Strangely, I had not heard or seen anyone.

Already, snowflakes were accumulating on my windshield, so I decided it was time to go home. I was disappointed and prepared to leave when I heard a voice, in the very depths of my soul, a rich-toned, reverberating voice that was dynamic and full of life. His tone of voice irresistibly drew me in. I did not think about being afraid. His voice was warm and tender.

"I want you to write this down," he declared to me.

I shuffled through my cluttered purse, rummaging for a pen. The only thing I had to write on was the inside front cover of a paperback book I had been reading. I opened to the inside blank cover of the book and waited in anticipation. Within the next few sacred minutes, I wrote down what he instructed me to write.

"You know I have brought you through everything, and you are learning, growing, and gaining wisdom. The first level is to get to the top, and you did. The second level is to tell people how you got there."

"But what do I know, Lord?"

"So much more than many others do, and they are praying for someone to help them. You can. Cast your bread, knowledge, thoughts, struggles, joys, and pains."

"Where?"

"On the waters."

"Write what you have lived," he told me. I have taken you places I have not taken others. Show them the places we have gone, and share with them the lessons I have taught you."

I

FIRE STARTER

While the specifics of our personal journeys differ, the common factor of transformation is that we can no longer remain just as we are. We are required to change, sometimes radically.

February 2006

*I*t was 2:45 a.m. I had been up for hours, pacing back and forth between the living room and the bathroom, convinced I had come down with a bad case of stomach flu. I felt guilty at the thought of making an emergency call in the middle of the night, especially if it really was just a stomach bug.

Eventually, my pain escalated from awful to excruciating. I fumbled for my cell phone at the bottom of my pink-and-white pajama pocket and called 911. Bracing myself for what was about to ensue, I unlocked the front door and turned on the porch light. Within a few minutes, the fire department and ambulance pulled up in front of my home, their red emergency lights flashing in through the porch windows.

After a brief evaluation, I was positioned onto a stretcher and hoisted into the back of the ambulance. The driver maneuvered the ambulance with aggressive speed. His sheer driving boldness let everyone know that the siren wasn't a polite request to move.

Holding my stomach and writhing in pain, my breath came out in short and rapid spurts. The paramedic urged me to breath slow and steady. He soon placed oxygen nubs into my nostrils and wrapped tubing around my ears.

Before long, the ambulance pulled up to the hospital emergency room. Glass double doors swished open as I entered on the gurney. A team of nurses immediately gathered information from the paramedic and surrounded my bed, hooking me up to monitors and taking my vitals. Within minutes, a towering, silver-haired doctor pushed the curtain aside and approached my bedside.

"I'm Dr. Larson." He wore a long white coat with his name inscribed in blue on his breast pocket. "Show me where it hurts."

"Here," I cried, pointing to the area where piercing pain consumed me.

Eyeing me, he quizzed, "Do you have your appendix?"

"Yes," I howled.

"Do you still have your gallbladder?"

"Yes," I lamented.

"Get blood work, stool, and urine samples, he said to the nurse. "Schedule a CT with contrast."

"Have you had anything like this before?" he asked.

"No," I bawled, "nothing like this."

As I continued to groan, Dr. Larson examined me from head to toe. Finally, the results of my blood work and stool sample were back.

"Your white blood cell count is elevated. You also have blood in your stool."

I wasn't sure what all of that meant. Overcome with pain, I was desperately begging for relief. Within minutes, morphine was being advanced into my vein.

Exhausted and wrung out, I was in a haze as the nurse transported me to the third floor: internal medicine. At 5:45 a.m., nurses had assisted in transferring me to my freshly prepared bed. A nurse wearing a smiley-faced scrub positioned an IV pole next to my bed and hung several bags of medication.

"I see Dr. Larson has ordered further tests for you throughout the day. He will come by this evening to see how you are doing and review any additional test results that are back. In the meantime, try and get some rest."

It was late that night when Dr. Larson walked into my room. He sank onto the green-and-blue plaid couch, which sat underneath my hospital window. I watched him thumbing through the papers in my file. He had a kind face with deep laugh lines around the outer corners of his eyes. He looked tired.

"I suspected this diagnosis last night. After looking over your test results, scans, X-rays, and blood work, I am confident you have Crohn's disease."

I eyeballed him. "I have what?"

Dr. Larson repeated the words "Crohn's disease."

I was speechless no witty comeback or sassy retort—nothing.

"Your swelling and inflammation can be seen on the diagnostic imaging you had earlier today. Crohn's disease is an inflammatory condition in which the body's immune system attacks the digestive system."

"My immune system is attacking me?"

"Yes. It can cause destructive inflammation throughout your body," he explained. "The benchmark signs of Crohn's include diarrhea five-to-fifteen times a days, sometimes more—watery, bloody stools; severe pain and aching in the abdomen and intestines; extreme exhaustion; malnutrition; and anemia."

"But I haven't been sick at all until last night," I protested, sure that he had made a mistake.

Smiling at my naïve reaction, he laid a packet of articles on the table beside my bed and suggested I become informed about my diagnosis.

Always eager to please—even when I'm sick—I nodded.

"Your intestines are swollen and inflamed," he added. "That's why you are having so much pain."

"How did I get this?"

"Scientists believe that Crohn's disease is caused by a combination of immune system problems, genetics, or environmental factors."

I was too stunned to say anything.

Dr. Larson informed me he was placing me on antibiotics and -would be ordering a steroid called prednisone to treat my inflammation.

"I know this is difficult to hear," he said.

The tenderness in his voice caught me off guard, and tears began to roll down my cheeks.

"There is no cure for Crohn's disease yet," he said, "but researchers are diligently working on it. I have several patients with Crohn's disease. We'll get through this." As he walked past my bed, he gave me a reassuring look. "I'll see you in the morning."

I mindlessly picked up the remote from the table next to my bed and began flipping channels. I paused on the weather network, wanting a distraction from the long days' events. My ability to concentrate was gone as the broadcasters droned on about a snowstorm that would be bearing down on southeast Iowa within the next several hours.

"In a couple of days, life will be returning to normal," the anchor conveyed.

Returning to normal, I thought mockingly. Then I whispered, "Lord, what is happening?"

Seven days later, once my inflammation and swelling had gone down, Dr. Larson wrote my discharge papers and asked the nurses to schedule me for an appointment at his office. It was around noon when I left the hospital on this bleak-looking February afternoon. I felt rather bleak-looking myself. My presentation consisted of blue tennis shoes, blue pants with no elastic waistband (elastic would put pressure on my stomach), and a long-sleeved flowing top to keep my bloated stomach hidden from view. That was fine with me. I never was a four-inch-heels kind of girl anyway. I preferred to wear comfortable clothes. Underneath my long, flowing top, bruises of black, green, and purple had emerged on my colorless arms and hands as a result of phlebotomists drawing blood.

Within twenty minutes, I pulled into the driveway, thankful to be home. The familiar tick of the starburst clock that hung on my living room wall and the humming of the refrigerator in the kitchen felt like comforting companions. As I walked into the living room, I saw the skewed glass coffee table sitting at an angle from its usual position. I was sure the firefighters had needed to move it when they brought the stretcher in. My favorite mauve rug was in the corner, wadded in a heap. A pot of dried out, rancid spaghetti sat on the stovetop. I had planned to take care of that before the firemen came, but obviously, that never happened. I could barely breathe from the overpowering odor in the bathroom. I cracked the window and sprayed Lysol over the sink and toilet, closed the door, and collapsed into my chair in the living room.

Wasn't it not long ago I was walking up and down stairs, crossing the campus to my graduate classes at St. Ambrose

University? Didn't I just spend hours shopping with my daughter, laughing, and stopping for something to eat?

How could all of this be happening?

REFLECTIONS

Crohn's disease is a taboo topic rarely discussed in an elevator or anywhere in public. It doesn't even get considered in many households in private. It is often diagnosed late because of the resistance to discuss it.

From the very beginning, Crohn's proved to be more than anything I had supposed myself capable of tackling. I knew God had plans for me, but the "getting through" part was and is hard. I stepped into the fog of sickness, and the rest of the world was lost.

It is misty now, but the fog will rise, and I will be able to see what was there all along.

I found the following quote as I was beginning my journey. It reassured me to know the Creator was not caught off guard by my diagnosis, even though I was.

Whatever has happened to you was not when he had his head turned.

He was looking straight at you.

—R.T. Kendall

2

SOMEONE IS CRYING

Our lives are a series of entrances and exits,
beginnings and endings, turning points of change.

$\mathcal{A}$s I was preparing for bed around 10:00 p.m. a few nights later, the sky was flawless. The stars were like fairy lights strung together in the heavens.

I put my head on my pillow with the physical and mental relief of putting another day behind me and a vague awareness of the duties that tomorrow would bring. After squirming and tossing for hours, I looked at the clock. It was long past 1:00 a.m.

I was seeing Dr. Larson in the morning and still taking prednisone (which causes insomnia) as well as another steroid, budesonide, used to treat moderately active Crohn's disease. The budesonide was to help keep the symptoms of the disease from coming back. (I took sixteen budesonide pills per day, plus all of my other medicines. Ugh!) My hope was that Dr. Larson would remove prednisone from my repertoire of medications. I was ready to be off of it!

After several hours of fidgeting, I heard the Lord's recognizable voice speak to me. "Can you hear someone crying?"

I rifled through my thoughts, explored my feelings, and hunted for the answer to his question.

While it was still hours before dawn, the answer became clear. "I know who is crying."

"Tell me," he urged.

"I am crying. I am crying for the loss of me and the life I loved. I am crying for my unfulfilled dreams."

"Yes," he spoke softly. "You can't follow me to where I am taking you if you are carrying your old baggage. Don't compare yourself with who you were. Who you were is not who you are."

Picking up a book from off my nightstand, I turned to a worn page.

William Bridges, in his book *The Way of Transitions*, writes about his wife, Mondi, who had breast cancer. "Every day I exchange who I thought I was with who I am now, she says. You are constantly letting go of who you thought you were and how your life would be. As she struggled along, day by day, for more than two years, she progressed from being simply a sick and frightened person to being someone who found a great deal of meaning in her sickness and uncovered new depths within herself because of her discoveries."

I was comforted by his wife's statement: "letting go of who I thought I was." I knew I was grieving over the loss of so much in my life. I was saying farewell. But letting go does not happen magically overnight.

In the coming days and weeks, I found myself humiliated. So many tears were held tightly in my heart for how I looked now compared to how I used to look. My new physical appearance startled me. I had developed a moon-shaped face (due to the prednisone). I hobbled when I walked and now had the need for a cane or walker. Where was the strong person I knew? During those hard days, I felt suspended, dangling between my old life and stepping into a new life.

"Birth is traumatic," the Creator told me. "It is the separation of past habits." Transition involves relinquishing the old habits and expectations and developing new ones that fit the new situation."

I anguished over what I wanted to do with my life against what I was physically able to do. My life changed when I got sick. It hurts to accept this truth. I will never be the same person again.

Give me some time, I assured myself, *and I will learn to live with the limitations.*

Early one morning I attended the sunrise as the dawn appeared in streaks of rose and pink across the eastern sky. I wondered if my pain and loss would serve any purpose. Could all this loss possibly serve as my call to a new way of life?

I thought of a passage from the book, *Make God Your Senior Partner* by Thor Hollbowich: "All great work for me is done in the individual soul of the worker."

Reflections

Crohn's is a disease of shame for most people.

Anything that deals with one's bowels is a hush, hush, conversation that makes the individual with the disease feel isolated, lonely, and full of despair. In 2015, over three million people in the United States were suffering with irritable bowel disorder.*

How do I experience the pain of life and face the darkness where nothing is clear or settled, where everything is shifting and changing?

In human brokenness, new life is born. Change is an indication God is doing something in your life.

Yes, the sun is coming up. How slow it seems when you are waiting on it, yet slowly, intentionally, and purposefully, something is happening.

3

ABLAZE WITH THE PRESENCE OF GOD

Jesus rarely comes where we expect Him.
He appears where we least expect Him and always in the
most illogical connection.
— Oswald Chambers, My Utmost for His Highest

---

*B*ack in the hospital the fourth time in two months, I woke to the pungent smell of hospital disinfectant invading my nostrils. My room was silent apart from the *beep beep* you hear in a hospital that indicates you're still alive.

There was no loud talking in the hallways, no cleaning crews pushing their workstations around, and no phlebotomists searching for patients who needed blood

drawn. Not in my most far-reaching imaginings did I suspect that on this morning I would experience a taste of life beyond my own.

I strained my eyes to see a man standing in the doorway. It was hard to make out his features. Initially, I thought he was someone arriving to take my vitals or bring my medication. He was not there to do any such task.

Crossing the threshold, the man then walked toward my hospital bed. He wore no golden crown on his head. No choir of angels was singing in exultation, heralding his entrance. He drew no fanfare or undue attention to himself. His clothing was opposite from how the familiar images had represented him. Dress and time seemed irrelevant. Strangely, it did not occur to me to be afraid.

As he approached, I instinctively knew him. As he came nearer to me, a deep peace permeated my soul.

A small smile played across his lips.

My cells were invigorated as he stood by my bed. Energy flooded through my body at the knowledge that the Creator of the universe had entered my hospital room.

As he reached for my hands, his fingers touched mine, and our eyes met.

"I've come to see you. It's not everyone I come to call on personally." His voice was reminiscent of a memory, as if returning something familiar to my soul. It was the richness in his voice, warm and alive, that sent a glow throughout my body.

He leaned over my bed, pressing his steady hand into mine. The touch of his fingers and the sweet smell of his breath as he bent close to me filled me with delight.

"Since the beginning, before you were born, I assigned you a destiny. Your destiny has prevailed throughout the ages. Now is the time for your purpose to begin stirring. Everything I am about to show you is my best for you. I would like you to come with me to one of my favorite landscapes," he said, sweetly summoning me.

"Come with you? How can I?" In bewilderment, I looked at him, then at the IV in my arm and the medicine bags hanging from the nearby pole.

He placed his fingers gently over the top of my lips.

"If you come with me, you will be able to see and listen to what I have to share with you. There will be no pain or suffering while we are entering these landscapes, and I will return you to this exact room when we are finished. Will you come with me?" he asked, extending his hands.

I looked at him, totally taken aback. This was mind-blowing.

"I understand this is confusing," he said, smiling down at me. "Yet I often step through doors into the hospital rooms of infants and children and embrace them in my arms. I move into intensive care units, whispering reassuring words that I am near." A wide smile broke out across his face as he shared with me how he sometimes sings with those who are comforted by a song.

"I reassure the dying, embrace the lonely, and provide hope to the hopeless. Now, I have walked into your room. I want us to talk about many things, including my primary purpose for coming, which I hope you will consider."

I looked at him questioningly.

"I am not an observer in your life, my child, I am a participant in your life. People diminish me when they see me only as the Creator, or Protector. I have limitless components. I AM bigger than a holy God. I come in humanness as well. The mechanics of how I do things is not the most important thing for you to know. What is important to know is that ever since I came to earth as Jesus Christ, I am able to be present with you personally."

Then he added, "It is true, this assignment will change you. But if you come with me, there are wonderful lessons to learn."

My mind assured me I must be delirious; my heart assured me I was not.

"Don't be afraid. It would be best for you to see things differently."

He extended his hand out to me again. And for the first of many times, I placed my hand in his.

Reflections

I often wonder why the Creator walked into my hospital room and came to me in the way he did. In my moments of uncertainty and despair, he knew what was best for me.

He knows one approach does not fit all of us, yet one Jesus fits us all. How is that possible? He comes individually, personally, and uniquely to one person at a time. It's what Jesus does; he comes near when your life is falling apart.

4

FIRE AND WATER

Save me, O God, for the waters have come up to my neck.
Do not let the floodwaters engulf me or the depths swallow
me up, or the pit close its mouth over me.
— Psalm 69:1, 15

When I opened my eyes, I found myself on the shore of a great lake. I glanced over at the Creator, and he returned my gaze with a reassuring expression. He grinned as we sat down side by side.

A sandy beach lay in front of us. Gentle waves were curling over and falling as they reached the shoreline. The soft sound of the waves in rhythm lapping up upon the water's edge was calming. The sun warmly shown overhead.

Slipping off his sandals, he dug his bare brown feet down into the tiny grains of sand. He motioned for me to do the same. The sand felt damp and warm as I pushed my feet down.

Turning toward me and looking into my eyes, he spoke. "I'm glad you came with me. I have brought you here as I have many things to reveal to you."

I sat close, watching him, listening to his words.

"Look around you," he gestured expansively. "It is a season of abundance."

Looking down the shoreline, I saw no other people on the beach. The seagulls were preforming their aerobatics far out over the lake. I breathed in deeply the aroma of opulent, lush orchids, red geraniums, lilacs, orange and red poppies, and roses of all colors and sizes. Each flower and fragrance added to the striking scene surrounding the calmness of the lake. Looking toward my right, I saw a small path that meandered around the lake.

White and yellow daisies fluttered and danced in the soft, warm breeze. I stared and stared at them, mesmerized. They seemed to be nodding to me as if to say, *Accept your destiny. It is his best for you.*

"All nature is a living landscape. I am the architect," he said. "Nature reveals me. I set all of life and growth into motion—the earthly world and the distant stars."

I watched his expression as his gentle yet steady eyes scanned across the lake, the trees and onto the distant, snow-covered mountains.

"I have an invitation for you to consider," he said tenderly. "Each one of my children has a special offer, custom designed by me, specifically for them. Although each person has a purpose, most need some preparation to accomplish their destiny. I must work with them before I can work through them."

I nodded. I had long felt the stirrings of destiny and purpose.

"Your assignment," he said, "will involve your transformation. I am asking you to become more like me. My children have the free will to choose to accept their purpose or not. If you accept, your journey will transform you into the person who has her eyes opened."

"And if I don't?" I asked timidly.

"I will always be here for you. That will never change. The choice is up to you. If you choose to remain in the life you have known, I will be here with you, as I always have been. If you choose the pathway to your destiny, you will step into a life that is my best for you. The choice is yours," he repeated. "Will you accept my assignment for you? Are you willing to be changed completely?"

"How can I be given an assignment now? I am in the hospital. I have a lifelong disease with no cure."

It was then my eyes became fixed on an ancient oak tree positioned not far from us. This towering tree was bursting with green leaves. Aware that I was focusing on this massive tree, he warmly said, "This tree is strong and filled with energy. It is a testament to endurance. It has been buffeted by winds that strike repeatedly and violently. It's been battered over and over and pummeled from side to side. It has been in squalls with low clouds and driving rain. Soon you will appreciate what nature can reveal to you." He rose from the sand and walked a short distance to the water's edge. Reaching the water's border, he stepped in and began walking away from the shore, out to the deep water.

I watched as the water rose to his knees, climbed to his waist, and finally reached his chest. Turning around, he gestured for me to join him. Pushing myself up off the sand, I reached the water's edge. With some trepidation, I stepped in as he had done and began walking forward, taking one step after another. Soon the water rose to my knees and climbed to my waist. As the water deepened, my fears began to intensify.

I slowed my steps as I approached him. The water was now slapping under my chin. If I took another step, the water would engulf me. *Can this be the same man who stood beside my hospital bed?* I wondered as I stood frozen with fear. *Is this the man who encouraged me to come with him? Why has he brought me here? Why is he asking me to do this? My thoughts raced as I panicked.* Another step and the water would completely swallow me.

Suddenly, I realized what was taking place. *He has brought me out into the deep water to make a choice. Will I accept his best for me, his plan for my destiny, or will I return to the life of familiarity?*

I remained motionless.

The Creator called my name. I understood I could turn around and walk back to shore without any rebuke, reprimand, or repercussions. If I pushed past my fears by taking one more step closer to him, though, the door would open to his best will for me.

"I want you to be more like me," he had said. In my heart I knew he loved me and did want his best for me.

For a moment I considered turning back toward the shore. I knew I had a choice to make, and only I could make it. Looking into his loving eyes, I drew in a deep breath and stepped forward. Immediately I was plunged below the water's surface into the bottomless lake. I instinctively thrashed to free myself, but no matter how hard I tried to emerge, it was impossible. Water flooded into my nose, ears, and mouth. My arms and legs were flailing as I beat frantically. I tried to stand, fiercely fighting my inevitable drowning. The heavy weight of the water held me down. I fought to push the water away from me. The need for oxygen was evident as my energy began to wane. I thought, for a moment, that perhaps my dying was his best for me.

In the next second, I felt his mighty hands reaching down to take hold of my limp body. I could feel the strength in his arms drawing me up from my watery grave. I resurfaced, gasping for air.

Tenderly, he caressed my wet, dripping face in his hands and said, "My child, surrender is a choice of the heart."

As we sloshed back to the shore, I considered his words.

Surrender is a choice of the heart.

The only sounds I heard were the seagulls squawking overhead, water splashing against our legs, and the declaration of the Creator's laughter.

Once on shore, he stood facing me. Reaching for both of my hands, he spoke, "I am asking you to accept the uncertainty of your life right now. Don't make your sickness your enemy. Know that your future is not uncertain to me. Don't fight; instead, embrace."

Holding me closely, he encircled me with his arms. He then stepped back, looked directly into my eyes, and said, "You have made a choice to accept what is my best for you."

I nodded yes, and he beamed.

Shortly afterward, we sat down on the warm sand and let the gentle breeze blow dry our hair and clothes. The sun hugged us as we sat together on the beach.

After a long interlude of silence, he turned to me said, "I want to build you a sandcastle."

I grinned spontaneously. Together we dug a self-replenishing water hole, which brought water to our building site. His hands began stacking handfuls of wet sand and tamping it down. I started to do the same.

"Pounding the sand into submission is a method of strengthening it," he said as he continued pounding.

I knew he was using the sand to illustrate what would be required to rebuild me.

Before long, the waves were nudging closer to the sandcastle.

"Transformation doesn't come without demolition," he quietly spoke. "Demolition is uncovering the person you are meant to be."

As the sun in the western sky was beginning to set, glorious hues of copper, orange, and red appeared upon the snow-covered mountaintops far off in the distance. Glancing over at him, he returned my look with a reassuring expression. Taking my hand in his, we departed.

Later that evening, in my hospital bed, I thought about what had happened today.

The Creator revealed his majesty through a visit to a lake where he asked me to surrender myself, and I did.

As the night nurse entered my room, she hung fresh bags of medication on the pole beside my bed. She took my vitals and evaluated my ankles and feet for any swelling. As she was nearing the end of her exam, she looked at me in amazement.

"Where did you get this sand on the bottom of your feet?"

Reflections

Love flowed like sweet nectar between us. It held the deliciousness of wisdom and the delicacy of understanding. I would come to discover that His love poured out whether I was good or bad, sarcastic or gentle.

During our times together, he was introducing me to love.

5

THE FIERY TRIAL

You need not cry very loud; He is nearer to us than we think.
— **Brother Lawrence**

I had seen Dr. Larson on Tuesday. My Crohn's symptoms continued to escalate. Diarrhea and debilitating pain made basic daily functioning nearly impossible. I was working extremely hard to keep myself from sliding down into the pit of despair.

"Come with me," the Creator said one early afternoon, and immediately I placed my hand in his.

At once, I realized we had returned to the lake. It was tranquil, like pure glass. The sun was warm, yet the air had a nip to it. We sat down near the identical spot we had been before. This time I could see all around the lake. Trees were sparkling with brilliant colors of watermelon red, lemon yellow, and bright orange. The hills were ablaze with color.

"The early turning species lost their leaves last week," he said. He pointed to the stand of trees by the path. "Many of the sugar maples are losing their dazzling orange leaves. The trees are showing us how lovely it is to let the dead things go."

"Let the dead things go," I repeated. I could feel my old self drifting away.

"Every season of life calls on a different dimension of the self." The Creator turned toward me, and I looked into his eyes. "Accept the help of your struggles and trials. These struggles and trials are not your enemies, although your predators want you to see them as enemies."

"Why?" I asked.

"If satan can convince you that nothing good ever happens to you, if he can keep you discouraged, beaten down, and depressed, no transformation happens. This is his goal: to keep you paralyzed and stuck."

I had thought about asking this question to the Creator before, but now I was finally ready. "Help me to understand why you don't heal me? People came from villages or towns and brought their sick, and whoever touched you became well. You have the power to heal me, so why don't you?"

"I could heal you, but if I did, you would never be able to have your eyes opened or develop into the person you are meant to be."

I thought of one of my favorite passages from Margaret Clarkson's book *Grace Grows Best in Winter*: "If God has entrusted you with a hedge of suffering, let Him teach you how to live within it so that His holy purpose and His life-giving fruit may be fully accomplished through you!"

I heard the Creator whisper, "Will you relinquish your identity in exchange for the new you? Will you climb on the altar? Nothing has changed according to my plan for you." Smiling warmly, he extended his hand. "Let's take a walk."

I enthusiastically put my hand in his. We walked side by side on the pathway. It was hard to decide which was more vibrant, the changing colors of the autumn leaves or the remaining clusters of purple and bronze mums and golden marigolds that were still randomly blooming along the path. We saw a few geese and ducks dunk their heads deep into the water for a buffet, their butts wiggling in the air. Flocks fluttered and scattered as they heard our arrival.

In due course, the path veered off toward a slender piece of land extending out into the water. We sat down on some brownish prickly grass. Looking skyward, I noticed the skies had been swept clean of white, fluffy clouds. I watched as the atmosphere became full of dark, churning thunderclouds. Rumblings and peals of thunder crowded the air. Like a whirlwind sweeping through the land, I soon heard unworldly sounds shrieking from the heavens. The sun hid from view. Terrified, I shielded my ears with my hands. I glanced over at the Creator. His countenance was as peaceful as when we first arrived.

Thunderously wicked screams permeated the air. Frantically, I searched for the source of the evil screams. It was then I witnessed it, an enormous, ominous form emerging from out of the raging lake and materializing directly in front of me. Masses of long, black, spikey braids with grotesquely twisted cords dangled from the writhing shoulders of this apparition. The spirit swung above the waters, its form hovering in the air, preparing to lunge at me.

Horror-struck, I staggered to my feet and began to run. As I bolted away from the apparition, I ran as fast as I could. Soon, I realized there was no place for me to hide. I ran farther away, then heard the Creator loudly exclaim, "If you keep

running from death, he will demand more and more of you."
As the Creator's words reached my ears, I eventually slowed
down and turned around. The mysterious, monstrous beast
had vanished.

Weeping, I staggered, trembling back to where the
Creator was seated. I was terrified this horrific form would
reappear and move toward me again. Once I arrived back,
I stood over the Creator, who was still seated. Without
hesitation, I looked unswervingly into his eyes.

Shaking, yet clear and resolute, I erupted. "I do not
want to do this assignment. I do not want to be created into
your best for me. The price is too high, and the agony is too
enormous." My eyes crowded with tears as I continued. "I
want everything to return to the way things used to be." My
voice was quivering as I shared my heart. "I want to be the
way I used to be."

Exhausted, I dropped down on the sand. The Creator
sat, calmly listening to me. At long last, he spoke. "This
aberration was the accuser's way to terrorize and intimidate
you. He attempted to bring to an end your desire to take hold
of your destiny." Fondly observing me, he asked, "Why did
you run?"

Frustrated with such an obvious question, I retorted, "If death catches me, I will die. I don't want to die."

For a long time, I sat down on the sand with fear and foreboding as my companions. In no time at all, resentment slithered into my thinking. Why had the Creator not annihilated this fiend and shielded me? Why did he allow the death angel to pass above me, descending closer and closer over my head?

How could this be his best for me?

A bitter coldness wormed its way into my heart, like the mysterious, strong waves still hammering the shore directly in front of me. I felt angry and disappointed. Though I was sitting near the Creator, I was not near him at all. I contemplated my sacrifices and suffering and the price I was paying for my destiny.

"It seems like I have to surrender and lose myself again and again."

"No," he said with a smile. "When you surrender, you find yourself."

I began to think that if he allowed death to come so near, what else might he permit? I questioned if I could even trust someone who determinedly sat still while I was terrified and filled with doubt. I saw no way this encounter with the death angel could ever be salvaged.

It was then he moved closer to me. "Let me restore your hope. I will never leave you, even though at times it may seem like I have."

If he thinks his words are sufficient to make up for not protecting me, he is wrong, I thought. Unexpectedly, I saw his hand reaching for me. I was not yet ready to grasp his hand in return. This incident had felt like a betrayal to me. He slowly kept extending his hand toward me. Looking into his eyes, all I saw was love. There was no scolding, no reprimanding, no sarcasm. I thought of his words the first time we had been to the lake: *surrender is a choice of the heart.*

"My child, if you did not love me, you would not be frustrated or struggling. The choice would be so much easier; you could just quit. But your love for me and your desire not to disappoint and hurt me is stronger than the struggle. You love me now more than ever."

My heart shattered as I remembered who it was that was reaching for my hand. I had to believe that he knew what was best for me. It was then I extended my hand to his. Even as our fingers touched, my hope rose.

Looking compassionately yet directly into my eyes, he said, "If you hold onto me, you will not need to run. When you hold onto me, the enemies retreat. Hold onto me, my child," he encouraged, "I am always here." Shifting himself even closer to me, he had a soothing presence. "Let's sit here awhile. The sun will be setting soon."

That evening, I had never seen a sunset where the sky burned so fiery red as that night at the lake with the Creator. We sat by the lake, watching the beauty of the yellow moonlight reflecting across the calm water. I loved the peaceful, soft sounds of the lake with its gentle waves bowing down to their maker as they reached the shore. The golden reflection of the moon created a path on the quiet lake. It was then time to return.

Reflections

There are times I had more faith than at other times. This was not one of those "more faith" times.

Can God's love hold me when everything says that his love is a lie?

This ordeal damaged my previously vibrant relationship with the Lord. I lived in apprehension, wondering when the other shoe would drop.

I continually found myself choosing my own will over His purpose for me.

Initially, the first drops of His love toward me splashed on the ground. Yet the Creator continually deposited into this nearly dead receptacle droplets of love that penetrated my heart and mind. His love passed through the walls I had built for protection. Every drop of love removed a little despair, a little hopelessness, a little pain, and I soaked it in. His love drops were moisture to my soul. Drop by drop, he lubricated my deadness.

Surrender is not a one-time decision, it happens again and again, but always, it is a choice of the heart.

6

FIRE AND ICE

God delivers some from circumstances and some through circumstances. — **Terri Sullivant, The Divine Invitation**

So many endings were occurring. I tried to step back into the Christian counseling company I founded in 2000. The company had grown and expanded. I longed to remain working, yet found myself paying a high price when I tried to.

One afternoon, after being released from the hospital and back at home, I drew out of my desk drawer a tan folder with the business logo I had chosen when I first started the business. My fingers rubbed over the texture of the file. I recalled making the decisions regarding the color, font, and quantity. As I began to open the folder slowly, I hastily closed it back up. My old life was in this folder—my joys and tears, laughter and pain, decisions, and heartbreaks. I let the folder lay on my lap for a while, then finally slid it back into my drawer, unopened.

"You can't follow me to where I am taking you, carrying your old baggage into a new place," He had told me. I never opened the folder again.

A few days later, I sat on the edge of my hospital bed, willing myself the strength to stand. I stood and began walking, then noticed that when I had slid out of my hospital bed, a trail of blood followed me into the bathroom. Exhausted, I leaned on the doorframe for support. Rich, dark blood streamed down my legs, past my knees, and onto the tops of my feet. I pulled the red emergency cord hanging near the toilet.

"Oh, honey," the nurse moaned as she stepped into my room, paging other nurses for additional help.

Eventually, I was positioned on a shower chair while warm water streamed over my body, washing my blood down the drain. None of the medications I was taking for Crohn's Disease was alleviating my inflammation, swelling, diarrhea, bloody stools, and intense pain.

Dr. Larson entered my room the following morning, informing me of a drug called mercaptopurine. "Mercaptopurine, also known as 6-MP, is a chemotherapy drug used to treat cancer and autoimmune diseases," he advised me. (Crohn's is an autoimmune disease.) Specifically, it is used to treat acute lymphocytic leukemia, chronic myeloid leukemia, Crohn's disease, and ulcerative colitis. "Mercaptopurine is an immunosuppressant; therefore it will reduce your body's ability to fight off infections. I want you to think about this carefully," Dr. Larson had said. "There are serious side effects; you should do some research on this drug before we move ahead." When Dr. Larson left my room, I prayed earnestly.

I told myself to look at this new chemo medicine differently. This medicine is not a poison to destroy me; this is medicine to help me. Regardless, I found myself full of fear. It was as if I could hear his voice. He was saying to me, "Everything that is happening to you is part of my plan for you. Nothing surprises me; no medication is stronger than I am; no illness is bigger."

After two days of mounting pain, Darvocet, oxycodone, and prednisone could not get my pain under control. The following day, late in the afternoon, mercaptopurine began slowly entering my body.

"The nurses will be monitoring you every fifteen minutes," my nurse, Kathy, informed me. She also reassured me that Dr. Larson could be reached at any time if there should be a problem.

Two hours later I began to feel like I was on fire. I was sure I had a fever. My hair was wet, and my body was limp. I pushed the red call button, and Kathy came in immediately. She felt my head and dampened a cold washcloth, placing it on my forehead.

"I don't feel good, I told her. I feel like I am on fire."

Kathy took my temperature and instantly paged Dr. Larson. Dr. Larson was at my bedside without delay. He began a quick examination, first looking into my eyes. He asked Kathy to retake my temperature.

"Dr. Larson, she has a fever of 106 degrees."

Like a drill sergeant, Dr. Larson started barking out orders. As I lay there, my body began to shake.

"Call all the nurses and have them bring in buckets full of ice," commanded Dr. Larson.

The nurse brigade, in purple scrubs, started hurrying into my room, carrying gray plastic buckets filled with ice.

Countless buckets of ice were unloaded on top of me, burying my entire body. The nurses continued this routine for over an hour until Dr. Larson informed the nurses they could stop. Eventually, dry hospital sheets and a fresh grown replaced my soaked gown and wet sheets.

"Lord," I whispered, "I am very sick and afraid. I need you. I'm not sure I'm going to make it through this." It was then I sensed a familiar presence in my room as The Creator took my limp hand and caressed it in his.

"I am here," he whispered.

Worn out from my ordeal, I remember the Creator standing by my bedside but recalled little else until the following day. Throughout the late afternoon and night, nurses continually monitored me. In the morning, Kathy came to check on me. After a brief conversation, I shared, "To some, I may look the same as I always have, but after storms of this magnitude, I am not the same." She nodded.

Within several weeks of my experience with mercaptopurine, I was inaugurated into the "losing your hair" club. My hair began falling out in clumps. Dr. Larson said losing my hair was probably from the prednisone or mercaptopurine. (A heads-up would have been helpful.) Showers became a time of misery as chunks of hair would slide down my legs and lie on the bathtub floor, taunting me.

Before Crohn's Disease, living well was comfortable. I could get out of bed, take a shower, dress, fix my hair, and still have energy left to put gas in my car, dart into the grocery store, and head to work, all before 8:00 a.m. I thought nothing of it back then. Now, most days I find myself stumbling like a small child around the house. As I was coming out of the bathroom a few nights later, I glanced in the mirror. I saw sadness on my face that hadn't been there before.

There was no spark, no flame, and no fire in my eyes.

Reflections

Whenever God gives a promise, fear knocks at the door. Lord, protect my mind from fearful thoughts of what this disease will do to me. I am being pushed forward, squeezed out of the place I know into a place of uncertainty and fear.

I discovered the following passage online. Try as I might, I haven't been able to find the source, but it was so powerful I wrote it in my journal. It really made me think:

I Am Fear

I have known you since you first saw the light of day. I have prevented you from getting better positions in your work. I have kept you awake many times by giving you horrible thoughts about your future.

All I did was make you afraid to ask or apply for them. I quiet your laughter when I say you will soon lose everything. I shatter your confidence when you stand to give a speech. You stand their panic in your eyes, twisting in the wind.

Often, I have been able to drag you around like a rag doll. I don't control you completely yet, but that will be up to you.

Just tell me everything is going to be all right. That I'm not going crazy, that it won't always hurt this bad always. Somebody take hold of me and pull me back from the edge of falling into the abyss.

I did not want to accept that I had Crohn's. I tried to act the same as I always had. I denied it ignored it, and fought it, but the reality was I had it.

I found it almost impossible to recognize my illness and trials as his gift to me. That inside his gift was wisdom, knowledge, understanding, and discernment made sense in my head, but it didn't make sense in my heart.

"It is the gift of growing and broadening you and so much more. I have given you a living gift, which I placed inside you. Initially, the gift seems like a betrayal and that I am not what I say I am, but the real reward is buried deeper inside you. This gift is my plan for you. You are in the world to achieve something, a function that will contribute to your readiness to help others," he had told me.

7

THE LITTLE PITCHER

We have a tremendous treasure in Nature. In every wind that blows, in every night and day of the year, every sign of the sky, in every blossoming and in every withering of the earth.

— Oswald Chambers, My Utmost for His Highest

*I*t was May, and the earth was stirring. I was eager to be outside. I planned to inspect my perennials and get my fingers in the dirt. I grabbed my hoe from off the patio and hobbled toward the garden.

It had just been a week since I was released from the hospital with a C. difficile infection (a bacterium that can cause symptoms ranging from diarrhea to life-threatening inflammation of the colon) and fever. But the earth was warm,

and my desire to be in the garden was intense. It seemed like even the plants were shouting at me to come and play. Soon, however, I had to rest because I had no more energy.

Before long, my back gate opened and the Creator walked through. As he entered, he stopped to smell the dark purple lilacs near the entrance of my garden.

"My daughter, I want you to begin looking for the gifts I give you every day."

"Gifts?" I asked, puzzled.

"Yes," he said with a smile, "like the sun shining through your window, offering joy, or the birds singing. The sky, clouds, trees, wind, and stars all have a language if you are open to listening. Yet you throw away the joy and hope that nature is striving to give you for the worry of tomorrow."

I thought about his words. His voice was not one of blame. He was giving me gifts, but I had not recognized them. I had become so consumed by all I was experiencing that my pain was all I could see.

He grinned and took a seat in a lawn chair next to me. "Many people are familiar with this story, but it fits for you to hear." I listened as he spoke.

"There once was a king who loved to host lavish parties and entertain his friends. Elegant tables and chairs filled his ornate dining hall. The most beautiful linens, sparkling crystal, and stylish china were chosen for such events.

"The king especially admired a beautiful little golden pitcher. The small pitcher was always placed directly in front of the king during his elaborate parties. The little vessel was so proud to be able to hold twelve ounces of the king's finest cream. 'I love my little pitcher,' said the king to his cupbearer, 'but I am in need of a larger pitcher to be used for a greater purpose.'

"Knowing that the twelve-ounce vessel was too small, he called for the palace artisans to appear before him. All of the artists entered and bowed down low. The king looked at his skilled creators of art, especially his sculptors and talented painters. He then looked down at the little vessel he held so tenderly in his hands.

"Looking up at the king, the little vessel, spoke, 'I know I am very precious to you. I also know that you need a larger vessel to be molded as you see fit. My king, because of your great love for me and mine for you, I will lay myself down to be remade.'

"With the surrender of the little pitcher, the king gave orders for his precious vessel to be broken, molded, and shaped into a vessel that could accomplish more in the king's service."

After he told me this story, he said, "If that little vessel stayed the same, it would only have a small amount to give. But if the little vessel is broken and molded and shaped into a vessel that can hold more, then it has more to give away."

I nodded.

"My child, if the assignment is greater, you also have to be broken and molded and shaped to accomplish your assignment. It would not be love if I had given you this new assignment and let you stay the same. That would have caused you more pain and suffering. Love knows you have to grow to live out this assignment."

We talked about the little pitcher's willingness to be broken and molded to serve a higher purpose.

Daily I was reminded of my need to surrender.

Turning toward him, I probed, "Why can't I learn to quit resisting?"

"I'm glad you asked. Remember at the lake when I told you that surrender is a choice of the heart?"

I nodded.

"Many hearts feel that if they submit, they are weak, feeble, or vulnerable. In reality, when the heart surrenders, it takes more strength and more courage. It all has to do with what is inside your heart. Surrender is a choice, a decision of the heart. Take some time as you sit here, and consider what makes surrendering difficult. A surrendered heart is a precious thing."

As he walked toward the garden gate, he called back, "In my kingdom, a surrendered heart is recognized as a very wise heart."

Down deep in my spirit, I heard the Lord say to me, "When trials and suffering come, you don't overcome sickness or poverty or divorce, you overcome yourself. Your job is to overcome you."

Reflections

After listening to this story, I was better able to see that it was love that prompted the little pitcher to surrender. It is his love for me that will allow me to be stretched and molded into the vessel that will be able to accomplish his best for me.

> He was continually introducing me to love, and that love adhered to my soul.

> I have to learn to celebrate my small successes along the journey.

> I am comforted when he keeps returning to me even though my faith is small.

8

A FLICKER OF HOPE

God doesn't make all things new by changing the outside. He wants to remake the substance of our lives.
— **Roy Hicks, Jr.**

*I*n March 2012, I closed the doors to my beloved company. I could not continue to run a company when I was so sick. In April 2012, I packed up the life I had known in Iowa and moved to Cheyenne, Wyoming. My son, Nick, my daughter-in-law, Amie, and my granddaughter, Haley, lived in Cheyenne, as well as my daughter, Sara.

A few weeks after moving to Cheyenne, I stood in the living room of the lovely house I had leased. Mature trees dotted this older neighborhood. I asked God for a sign to let me know He was near.

Within minutes, a robin flew to the black rod iron railing on my front porch and sat there. Soon she began to sing. Later I would discover that the robin was building a nest in the tree next to my porch. As the afternoon slipped into the evening, I watched as the sun set in the West and streetlights on the corner flickered on.

Most of my belongings were placed in a storage unit while I was adjusting to a new state, a new home, a new climate (strong winds), new doctors, new weather, and new everything. That night, as I listened to the late news, a winter weather warning had been posted for five to ten inches of snow with high winds.

I wrote that night in my journal: "The wind is so strong here, and it seldom stops. That's what I want in my life, Lord, no wind." I looked out my window and saw the wavering trees. They weren't fighting the wind; they were simply going with it. If I fight everything, it just wears me out.

The following morning it was bitterly cold, negative thirty degrees. (It's Wyoming, after all!) My furnace was continually working, pushing warm air into my unfamiliar house. I sat and watched the sunrise in the east and the fumes streaming from cars and chimneys.

My walls are bare, with very few of my comforts from Iowa. My son brought me an oversized maroon recliner and placed it in my large living room. I had a small television and was able to find *The Waltons* on my TV, which was oddly comforting.

I had an adequately sized kitchen with new marble counters. A thoughtfully placed window over the sink allowed me to look out into my lovely backyard.

One afternoon in late May, a light breeze blew the scent of summer in my direction as I sat in my lawn chair in the back yard.

"Your backyard invites repose," he told me. "Relish the serenity. Rest has always been a problem for you."

He was so right. When things were tame, I was restless.

Once again, he reached for my hand, and I eagerly placed my hand in his. Instantly we were standing on the side of a multilane highway, watching as the traffic rushed by us. Large areas of pavement spread out as far as I could see. Futuristic high-rise apartment complexes rose skyward on either side of the freeway. Apartment structures and parking garages filled my view. Cascading water tumbled over boulders drowning out the sound of constant traffic.

"People live in the Land of Urgent," he explained. "The land is saturated with rushing, running, and racing. Living in this land causes the internal pressure to keep pushing. Beneath the roar of traffic, underneath the rapid pace of change, so many faces pass by unnoticed. So many of my children are dry and exhausted. They go about their daily routines emptied."

I knew what he was talking about. I had felt that way myself.

"Your lessons are not hurry-up lessons," he added. "Relax and embrace our time together. Come away with me, and you'll recover your life. I will show you how to take a real rest. Walk with me and work with me. Watch how I do it. Learn the unforced rhythms of grace. Sometimes, my gifts to help my children do not seem like a gift at all."

I know, I thought.

"You think you are useless. You believe there is no meaning or purpose in your life."

I nodded.

"You are not useless. New experiences are a gateway, not an end. You are not starting from scratch again. You have not lost all you have learned. I would not give you the gifts you had before and take them away when you became ill."

It was as if he had read my thoughts and fears.

"For now," he added, "you are learning in the college of pain and suffering. Today, I want you to think about all that you are instead of all that you are not. Recognize you are being tenderly prepared for something you could not have done as your old self. Let rest rejuvenate your soul. Use nature as a resource. A heart at rest gives life to the body. Let nature become your friend and teacher. Feel the calmness nature gives you when on the inside you feel panic."

After our conversation, I intentionally began to search for joy. I bought a bird feeder and began to observe the small, yellow goldfinches returning to the feeder many times a day.

I placed a plant or a flower in my living room; it gave me joy.

"Assemble your favorite scripture, quotes, and inspiration," he encouraged me. "Give yourself permission to let go of all your worries. Ask yourself, Is this something I can control or not?"

At some point, I decided to transform my walker into a rolling university. What was stopping me from educating myself about the type of trees and plants I had never seen in Iowa. Many days I didn't feel like reading, thinking, or even moving, but on the days that I did, how much I enjoyed my mobile university. I often studied the color of the sky and counted the jets as they wove white ribbon plumes behind them.

All I could do some days was to crack a window so that some fresh air would come into the house. I moved my chair so that the sunshine would bathe me. (In reality, I had to have someone else move the chair.) I permitted myself to have do-nothing days. I came across a poem on one of my do-nothing days that brought me peace and calmness when everything else seemed to be in chaos.

> *My quiet days—a curtain's blowing grace,*
> *A growing plant upon a windowsill*
> *A rose fresh-cut and placed within a vase*
> *A table cleared, a lamp beside a chair,*
> *And books I long have loved beside my chair.*
> — **Author Unknown**

Reflections

How I fought to keep my grip on the life I had built. For an exceptionally long time, I could not understand why my whole life would have to be released. Then more storms came.

When I was a child and signs of a storm were marching toward our two-story farmhouse in Iowa, we scrambled down a half-dozen cracked cement steps into the musty-smelling cellar, our ears attentive to creaking boards and dangerous wind gusts. Mom or Dad would pull the cellar door shut as our family anxiously huddled together until the storm passed over.

Where do I run from the storms and the chronic despair of illness and the loss of everything I held so dear?

Filled with love and compassion, he tenderly reached for my hand. "Show me your wounds. I will take your wounds and scars and suffering and water the world."

9

LITTLE FIRES EVERYWHERE

Chronic inflammation is different.
The same reaction as in acute inflammation takes place,
except now the flame persists.

*D*r. Carter, my new gastroenterologist, was personable with a confident nature. He was young, small in stature, yet brought warmth and kindness into our visits. After reviewing my file as well as escalating hospital stays, Dr. Carter spoke with me about having resection surgery. Resection surgery, he explained, is a common form of surgery for Crohn's disease patients that involves removing the diseased part of the large or small intestine and then sewing together the healthy parts.

He was hoping that my resection surgery would allow my body to go into remission, a stage of Crohn's when your disease is no longer active. That means inflammation stops causing painful damage to your bowel and colon because your immune system is working as it should.

Three weeks later I had the surgery. When I was brought back into my room, the surgeon informed me he had removed thirteen inches of my large intestine. For the next three months I began to feel revived and noticed a tiny spark of hope. Heading into the fourth month since my surgery, however, I made an appointment with Dr. Carter and expressed to him I was not feeling well. I recognized the symptoms of Crohn's and told him I was sure my Crohn's disease had come back.

Dr. Carter had previously informed me that after a resection surgery, Crohn's could go into remission for a year or longer. He ordered blood tests, a colonoscopy, and scans. It was evident the medication I was taking was not working because the inflammation and swelling, diarrhea, and intense pain had returned with a vengeance.

Dr. Carter advised me that I needed to be on a biologic. Biologics are powerful medications, a class of drugs that suppress or reduce the strength of the body's immune system. Biological medicines tend to be at the cutting edge of research.

My first biologic was a tumor necrosis factor (TNF) blocker called Humira.

Monthly I drove to the infusion center at the hospital and received injections. Eventually, I learned to give myself the injections. Ultimately, though, I developed a bad reaction to Humira and began another biologic called Remicade. I received infusions of Remicade for nearly a year and a half before my body developed antibodies, forcing me to discontinue it. But while the Remicade was working, I felt so much better. It was amazing. I felt like a human being again.

I thought about creating birth announcements for myself!

While I was receiving Remicade infusions, Dr. Carter also made a referral to a rheumatologist. At my first visit to the rheumatologist, Dr. Jackson's nurse drew countless tubes of blood for testing. A few weeks after my initial appointment, I found myself back in Dr. Jackson's office. He walked into the corner office, where I was seated on a chair next to his desk, and began taking my blood pressure.

"We need to talk," he said.

Not a good sign, I thought.

"Your test results are back," he announced. "The results indicate you have lupus erythematosus, which mistakenly attacks healthy tissue. You also have rheumatoid arthritis, a chronic inflammatory disorder affecting joints, including those in the hands and feet. These diagnoses are in addition to your Crohn's disease."

Now I have three autoimmune diseases, I thought.

Driving home from my appointment, I was numb. I didn't know how to feel. The revelations about my health were overwhelming. Both lupus and rheumatoid arthritis are autoimmune diseases, as is Crohn's disease. Dr. Carter and Dr. Jackson informed me it was not unusual for people with autoimmune disorders to have a comorbid diagnosis.

Reflections

After these diagnoses, I had a long conversation with the Lord. I shared with him that this was more than I could carry. I knew very little about Crohn's disease initially. But I knew even less about lupus and RA.

It was during this season that the fluids, nutrients, and drugs entered my body intravenously, but his love was like sap dripping from the trees; it was continuous and with infinite quantity. During this grueling period, I found more courage than I ever thought I had.

10

FIELD WORK

God does not waste suffering. If He plows, it is because He purposes a crop. — **Isobell Kuhn**

I was restless as I laid in my hospital bed, looking out the window. Once again, I had been brought to the emergency room with excruciating stomach pain. However, this pain did not feel like the standard stomach pain I had come to recognize. After a CT scan, the hospitalist informed me I had an intestinal obstruction.

An intestinal obstruction is a potentially dangerous condition in which the intestines are blocked. Both the small intestine and large intestine, called the colon, can be affected.

When a blockage occurs, food and drink cannot pass through the body. When asked what causes an intestinal obstruction, I was advised it could be fibrous bands of tissue that form after surgery, an inflamed intestine (Crohn's disease), infected pouches in your intestine (diverticulitis), hernias, and colon cancer.

The emergency room nurses inserted a plastic tube into my nose, past my throat, and down into my stomach. Not fun! Per the doctor's orders, I was unable to eat anything. (Honestly, I didn't feel like eating anyway.) After several days, my swelling and inflammation began to subside, and I was allowed Jell-O and popsicles. Initially, even the Jell-O and popsicles made me sick. I was not released until I could eat soft foods. Because of this, it turned into an extended stay!

As I continued to remain in the hospital, one day I heard a voice I knew well. Excited to see the Creator, and before he even asked, I extended my hand. Instantly we were strolling on a gravel road, with a few potholes here and there. I breathed in a deep breath of warm air, and the sweet smell of dirt filled my nostrils. In the distance, I heard the heartening sound of cows mooing. Simultaneously, the guttural sound of a tractor cultivating dirt close by filled my ears. The ditches, on both sides of the gravel road, were filled with grasses, tall weeds, purple-headed thistles, milkweed pods, and an occasional cluster of yellow sunflowers and wild roses.

As we continued down the road, I could see a long gravel driveway with an aging two-story white farmhouse. A plow and hay wagon was parked efficiently next to the barn. A couple of timeworn corn sheds were progressively tilting. A tall windmill was making a rusty metal noise as it slowly turned. A five-wire fence with posts protected the animals and crops. We walked past a herd of Holstein cattle grazing in the field.

Pointing down the road, he said, "This is the road the farmers use to drive their farm equipment to work in their fields." Smiling at me, he continued, "What do you know about plowing?"

"I know a little about plowing," I replied with a smile.

"Let's get closer," he said as he headed toward the ditch.

Stepping down into the ditch, he took a few steps and jumped the fence so that he was standing right beside the plow. Navigating through the tall grasses, I walked to the fence, and he lifted me over it. I stood on one side of the plow, and he on the other.

Looking into my eyes earnestly, he said to me, "The plow is a breaking device. It prepares the field for its purpose.

The plow forces its way through the ground to break up the soil and turn it over. Time and again, the ground is hard and dry, and the soil must be loosened or broken up with a heavy machine. Before the farmer can reap the harvest, the field must be prepared for growing crops."

Reaching for my hand, he added, "You are that field" (1 Corinthians 3:9).

"Tell me more," I said.

Pointing toward the field, he continued, "That field cannot be used for its greatest purpose the way it is now. The soil has to be broken up and turned over into furrows. The ground must be prepared for the seed. Even though the field pleads with the plow to stop tearing into its tender flesh, the plow must keep going. The plow persists determinedly despite the obstacles. The plow is a gift, but at the time, it does not feel like it. If the field could see the vision I have for it, it would not be so resistant. You are undergoing the pressure of being plowed from underneath. Only my finest seed will be planted in a field that has gone through so much."

I began to understand all that the field must go through to prepare it for its highest use and that what I was experiencing was the preparation of myself so that I could produce a harvest.

"Listen to me." He stopped and turned toward me. "The plow turns over your mind to consider new perspectives, new possibilities, and different ways of handling difficulties. Once you have a turn of mind, your mind is in a different position concerning its surroundings. You are a newly plowed field, operating at a higher level, and better than what you were before. Listen to the earth. The most important work happens in the field." Then he looked at me. "I have something to ask you."

"I'm ready. Ask me."

"Can you find the highest meaning in your mission now? Can you see a pathway to developing a new destiny? The field may appear to be barren, but the future is being prepared beneath the surface."

Later that evening, I replayed his words about the field. What did his lessons about the field tell me? Was my ground hard and dry?

"You are the field," he had said to me. Were clods of resistance keeping my field from its purpose? Were there stones in my field?

"You are being plowed," he told me. "You are being remade, refined, and reformed."

The underground work is happening. Life is stirring below. His words took me to a place of better understanding. I was beginning to realize that for me to be my best, I needed to be more like him.

Pain is a sterile thing, but like the plow that bites deep into the winter-bound earth, releasing life-giving nutrients and allowing sun, air, and rain to penetrate, pain can prepare the way for fruitfulness.

Reflections

Perhaps it's because I grew up on a farm in northern Iowa or that I love to dig in the dirt and grow plants and vegetables that I relished our time together here. Our visit to the field spoke so clearly to me. There will never be a time when I pass a tractor in a field that I am not reminded of being plowed for the sake of renewal. Dirt is necessary for growth and development.

You have to push through the dirt.

II

FORGED IN THE FURNACE OF AFFLICTION

When you're in over your head, I'll be there with you. When you're in rough waters, you will not go down. When you're between a rock and a hard place, it won't be a dead end—because I am GOD, your personal God, the Holy of Israel, your Savior. I paid a huge price for you . . . That's how much you mean to me! That's how much I love you!
— Isaiah 43:2–4 msg

Things were tough. I had not heard anything regarding my application for disability, and I was worried.

One morning, the Creator said to me, "This sickness, poverty, and loss is your portal of entry into the next dimension. The tighter you hold on, the less I can pour into

you. Let me pour more of myself into your new life. I could instantly hold the rain or stop the trees from budding. I could tell the birds not to sing, but all are my ways of showing you my love. Let go and let me handle all of this."

I checked the mail every day, looking for a letter about my disability. I was down to $8.35 in my checking account, and still I heard nothing.

One late afternoon, I received a call from Joan, a lady who worked at the Disability office. She called to say I had been approved for disability. I don't remember anything else she said. I know I asked her to repeat that I was approved several times.

"Thank you, Lord," I kept repeating. "Thank you."

Poverty comes in many forms. I knew this. I had been a social worker for twenty years and saw firsthand the effects of poverty.

"Life is not always big things and successes," the Creator told me. "Life is accepting where I have you. Work is being done, although in the visible you may not see it."

It took every ounce of courage I had to walk into family services and talk with them about food stamps. I had never used a SNAP card before (a card that looks like a credit card for those who need food assistance). I was quickly approved, and a few days later the SNAP card came in the mail. I was worried that the card wouldn't work, or the pin number that family services gave me for the card would not be the right one. It may seem silly, but the courage it took to use my food stamp card was gargantuan.

I had a master's degree in social work for Pete's sake. I used to have my own successful company. How could I be holding a food assistance card in my hand? I had put much thought into my strategy of going to the grocery store for the first time, using my card. I chose the time of day when there would be the least amount of people in the store because I felt so ashamed. I looked for a cashier whose line was not too busy because of my humiliation. I decided I would only buy a couple of cheap items. If the card didn't work, then I wouldn't be so embarrassed. (It was logical at the time.)

I prayed for hours before I walked into the store. To my great relief, everything went smoothly, and the next morning I went back to the grocery store and filled my grocery cart with groceries. The joy I felt leaving that store with food was tremendous, but the pure pleasure of unpacking my groceries and filling my cupboards was beyond belief.

After qualifying for food stamps, I was now eligible to see medical doctors who took Medicaid. Before meeting the requirements for Medicaid, all of my doctor appointments, hospital stays, tests, and medications were accumulating in a finance office at the hospital and at several medical locations. I saw a variety of doctors weekly.

On one occasion, a taxi picked me up at my house (paid for by the state). I had no money to put gas in my car; besides, I had no insurance for my car and no tags for my car either. I was filled with shame. The taxi drove me to the housing authority, where I signed paperwork for Section 8 housing. When my name was called out loudly by the receptionist, I wanted to dry up and disappear.

"Can you imagine you are richer now than before?" he asked me. "Richer in wisdom and in understanding. Richer in learning to depend on me."

Reflections

Suffering has a way of exposing our theology, certainly our practical theology, where what we believe about God collides with where we live.

Every experience changes you: accidents, death of a loved one, illness. You are not the same on the other side of them.

During this time, I would sit out back on my small patio,

even in the winter months, watching the sparrows flitter around the bare branches of the mature oak tree. I breathed in the crisp, cold air and purposely worked to find joy.

"Don't settle for less and less," he told me. "Where are your bigger plans? Use all you have been through."

12

I SAW LOVE

In addition to feeling sick and tired, I also felt forgotten, and there was no easy cure for that. — **Sandra Siemens**

*C*rohn's is such a lonely, isolating disease that even the slightest smile or touch from someone can make a difference.

My family often stopped at the house, texted me, or called to see how I was feeling. They would bring me groceries or my medicine or whatever I needed, and we would catch up on the latest in their worlds and in mine.

One day, I needed to go to the grocery store for a few things. Grabbing a grocery cart, I rested on it as I moved slowly up and down the aisles. It was then, unexpectedly, I

saw love. A lady I did not know looked at me and smiled. Such a small thing, an unexpected smile, but it warmed my heart. Over and over again, I felt removed from the stream of humanity, isolated and alone, but on that day her smile was a drop of love on a dead thing, and it brought life.

Who would get so excited about a smile? I knew she recognized my situation. The situation I was enduring was not specific to just me. Others are in similar situations too. Many people are going through things worse than mine; multitudes are lonely, overwhelmed, isolated, and withdrawn. Her acknowledgment of me felt like a form of love, of shared humanity. Without love, there is no life in us. We are dead! No love, no life. Little love, little life. Much love, much life. One drop of love creates life. One drop of love to a broken person or child makes you a life-giver, just like the Creator himself.

The next time I saw the Creator, I asked him about love.

"Why would you use such a fragile vessel to pour such valuable content into? Why would you not choose a robust and sturdy container to hold this treasure?"

He replied lovingly, "Strong, sturdy vessels hold onto love, and the contents of their containers become old and stale. They are fearful someone will take a drink or a drop of love from their vessel, so they protect the vessel at all costs. Emptied out, spilled over, cracked, and broken vessels have gone through the fire, been ground down, and then crushed until they are like fine dust. The kingdom language is not about holding onto love. It's about letting go and being filled with the contents of new birth, a new beginning. And without love, there is no life in us."

Reflections

I thought for hours about that woman's smile. Such a small thing with such a significant impact. I wondered if she had been through illness and recognized the signs in me.

Knowing the effect her smile had on me helps me to smile at others when I see them at the stores.

I know that changing clothes or getting a ride to the doctors office or considering how much money to spend on the items you need most, especially when you have so little, all take effort. A smile is a little thing to give to someone else—a little droplet of love.

13

THE UNDERGROUND WORK OF THE CAVE MUST BE DONE

Everyone has their own cave with the issues the devil knows will destroy them. Each cave is unique. But never will I forget the flames that consumed my faith.

The Creator led me along a path that often seemed too bewildering and difficult to be possible. As time passed, I had gone through several biologic medicines that worked for a while but then lost their effectiveness, or my body developed antibodies, which meant I could no longer take that drug. My pain was relentless. My hope was nearly gone.

My future became a blur. I worked hard at keeping myself from falling into the pit of despair, yet I was completely empty.

I was frightened and fearful of what lay ahead. Usually his hand would be reaching for me. This time, I entered my cave alone. The cavity was large enough that some portions of the cave did not receive any direct light (fitting for where I was at the time). The cave contained a maze of underground tunnels and narrow passages.

It was dark, but I was not cold. The cave was silent, but I was not afraid. The only sounds I heard were the thoughts in my head. Deep stillness surrounded me.

In those days of fear, depression, and hopelessness, the vast darkness of the cave defined me. I sat and stared, nearly unaware of time. I had no focus, no direction, and no connection to life as I had known it. I felt my identity being stripped away. *Do I still show signs of life?* I wondered I felt my faith weakening.

Depression robbed me of my voice. The enemies of fear, intimidation, poverty, sickness, and a mass of others came in numbers far greater than I could handle, and the Creator did not come to me.

I was getting smaller and smaller, and the Creator still did not come. If I stayed in my cocoon, not only were my autoimmune diseases stealing from me, but my depression and despair were robbing me as well. I was empty and confused as the tormenting questions concerning the Creator muddled through my mind.

Oswald Chambers, in his book *My Utmost for His Highest* says, "Watch when God shifts your circumstances and see whether you are going with Jesus, or siding with the world, the flesh, and the devil. We wear His badge, but are we going with Him?"

I felt as lifeless as a burial tomb. Through counseling, medication, nature, sermons, and quotes, the day finally arrived when I was willing to consider my choices.

I knew that it was essential to be gentle with myself. As with all difficult things, it was a process.

I began my internal dialogue with the following questions: *Who am I now? What am I accomplishing in this cave? When will I be ready to leave it? Where will I go when I come out of this cave?*

Over time I learned burial tombs do have something to reveal. The cave will not remain as it is. I will not remain as I am. In the narrow passages of the cave, I began to notice there was room after room of crystals that had been formed from heat and pressure. Was that what I was experiencing, the molding of me from heat and pressure? Crystallization is a purification step; once completed, the crystal has more value. The secret process of long ages of growth in the darkness was sprouting an awakening, a rebirth. I was being unearthed.

At long last, I was able to see walls on either side of the cave that would allow me a place to escape. I examined the mouth of the cave. It looked like an exhausting haul to the surface, but I began to climb out.

It was then I heard The Lord say to me, "I am bringing you out with a high hand. Everything you go through grows you. You cannot rush growth." Tenderly leaning down beside me, he continued. "How often I have wanted you to see that your illness, your battles, and your suffering are my gifts to you. In order to accomplish your purpose and complete the assignment, you had to uncover your own brokenness. Your old self would never have allowed you to see the real you. You had to be emptied of self, humbled in ways you could not imagine. Only when you surrendered your old self could your new self then move into your new heart. When you have been where the broken multitudes are, you can speak with authority."

I began to see my sickness as my gift; my enemies as my helpers; my weakness as my strength; my death as my resurrection. Slowly, new and beautiful thoughts began to push out my old sadness. Life had changed, not ended. Every new step I took required a new mentality.

Reflections

Suffering and crisis become our chrysalis, our home of transformation.

Depression is a difficult thing for many people to understand. I saw gentle and courageous warriors battling depression when I had my practice. Sometimes family, friends, co-workers, and church members think that depression is laziness. They become frustrated that the person living with depression doesn't simply "get over it." Depression doesn't work that way. Depression often comes from the masks we wear.

Never underestimate the pain of a person, because in all honesty, everyone is struggling. Some people are better hiding it than others.

Some of us give ourselves shots of methotrexate. Some of us give ourselves shots of alcohol. Both serve to numb the pain. One grabs her cane and weakly hobbles to her bedroom; one grabs her keys and heads toward her car. Both are suffering.

When God gets ready to see what's in you, he puts you in a dark place, buried in something designed to make you grow. This dark place is working for you.

During my time of darkness, depression, and despair, my psychological journey mirrored my physical journey. It was the undergoing of my journey that provided me with the capacity to conquer the challenges that seemed previously unconquerable. It's traumatic to be born.

14

THE WATERING PLACE

He led you through the vast and dreadful wilderness, that thirsty and waterless land. — **Deuteronomy 8:15**

*I*t was the middle of July. I was sitting outside on the cement porch steps in front of my house. It was too hot to stay inside, although it didn't feel much cooler outside. It was summer, and the weather had been blisteringly hot. Wide cracks had grown deep into the barren, parched soil. There had been no rain for months.

"Every person goes through times of drought. Everyone experiences dry seasons where nothing seems to be happening.

I have ways of making rain in your life that you have never dreamed of," he said, grinning at me.

The nape of my neck was damp as I lifted the frosty glass of water and melting ice to my lips. My skin felt sticky, and my blue tank top clung to me. How I needed a good soaking rain to bring life back to me. I was sure the parched gardens, the wilting flowers, and the panting dog rolling in the dust across the street needed a good soaking rain as well.

Even though it was late in the afternoon, the sun was still blazing down on my head. My mouth was dry and my tongue stuck to the roof of my mouth (partially due to my medication). I imagined myself feeling the fresh, clean wetness of rain as a cloudburst of water would unload its welcome contents directly over me. I wanted a downpour.

Later that afternoon, there was not a leaf stirring on the maple or elm trees. It seemed as if the entire row of trees in the neighborhood were standing motionless as sentinels. The sun became hidden by an enormous, dark cloud overhead. An eerie stillness had fallen on the land. I could see storm clouds massing. I tilted my head to listen, but even the birds were quiet. Off in the distance, a sizzling bolt of lightning streaked across the blackening skies. A continuous display of lightning flashes and rumbles of thunder hovered above.

Looking over at me, he said, "If there is no one to water you, I will water you. You are precious seed."

My instincts were now on full alert. I strained to listen. I smelled the rain coming before I felt it. I heard the rain before I touched it. At that moment, a single drop of rain plunked onto a dried maple leaf lying in front of me. Then another raindrop landed on the cement sidewalk near my bare toes. Before long, the skies split open and a deluge of heavy raindrops pelted the ground. I was filled with thanksgiving as the rain came down in buckets. It was as if the gates of heaven had opened, and every stored-up raindrop came bursting forth. The downpour brought joyful children out of their homes, dancing and splashing in the rain. Grown-ups stood in the downpour, refilling their tired, dehydrated bodies. The next morning, droplets of moisture dangled on the tree leaves and blades of grass.

"Wetness does not have to be moisture," he told me. "Wetness is a place that permits your soul to escape drought. What quenches your thirst?" he asked me. "That is your place of wetness. You need to discover your own watering hole."

"Watering hole," I pondered.

"Sure, it's a natural hollow in the ground that contains water. A watering hole is an oasis, a pond, or a spring. What is your water supply? How do you irrigate yourself? What is your delivery system?" Then he added, "Satan wants you to think you will always be dry and parched. That is not true. It is a strategy to increase your weakness."

"What am I to do?" I asked.

"Create a watering place, a refuge. Whether you find wetness in art, drawing, nature, or music, discover what your rain is, and go to it when you are dry."

The rain continued to seep into the soil for hours. *It's resurrection rain*, I thought to myself. That downpour of steady raindrops was watering my soul. I felt rejuvenated. I told myself to put out my rain barrels and pots and pans and collect his rain. The freshness of this experience in the rain gave me hope.

Reflections

My watering place comes from flowers, books, music, and writing. I started piano lessons when I was five years old. Even then, music watered my soul.

When I write about rain, the dry grass will turn green. The leaves on the trees will bud. The rain will soak down into the dormant seeds and cause them to awaken and drink in the rain.

What blessing do you think your Father wants to shower on you? It is through your watering place that comfort will come, fears will be minimized, doubts and uncertainty will flee, and peace and hope will pour into broken souls, replenishing their hearts.

15

THE SEEDS OF HOPE

Every seed destroys its container, or else there would be no fruition. — **Florida Scott-Marwell**

*W*hen I was young, my grandma and my mom would spend hours at the kitchen table looking through seed catalogs that came in the mail during the dead of winter in Iowa, giving them inspiration for the summer ahead. Burpee always had one of the most colorful catalogs and a wide selection of seeds. I remember how excited they would be to place their orders, counting the weeks until the seed packets would arrive in the mail.

"You are the seed," he told me. "Each seed pushes boldly, destroying the walls of its tomb. Think of the little seed in the hard ground. What a task beyond its power. The seed compels itself. You must plant yourself because unless the seed dies and goes into the ground, it can't bring forth fruit. Once the seed submits, life begins for the seed."

I knew he was talking about me being the seed.

"First is the surrender of the seed, which allows for growth. Then comes the bud, the stalk, the fruit, and finally the multiplication of the fruit to the world. A seed stays a seed unless its form and state of being change. As the grain of wheat falls to the ground, it lets go of what it is for what it can become."

He added, "Plant the seed of courage, the seed of hope, and the seed of love. The seed vessel, the container, must be broken off, exposing the embryo. Change is the stirring of the seed. Something has to change to awaken the seed within you. Without change, the seed remains dormant; therefore you stay dormant. Your seed is unbelievably valuable. Great sacrifice and suffering have birthed your seed. That is the reason you want your seed to be great. You can't take your seed and throw it out to be sowed. This seed has cost you your life."

I nodded.

He continued, "If you break yourself open, as the seed must, I will reveal my glory. Your seeds are indispensable.

They are priceless. Your fields are going to produce grain." He smiled and concluded with confidence, "You will need more grain bins."

Reflections

Held inside the protective coat, the seed is safe but numb. The time has come for you to take off your coat and lay it down.

I was planted in a very dark place. My seed went through a transformation only to come back up better than it was when it went down.

What has my seed cost me? Everything. I had to sacrifice something of myself to bring something back to life.

The resurrection seed is about to break forth and give you the desire to live again. You will discover the desire to love again, the desire to dream again.

16

THE GLORIOUS LEAF
OF HOPE

When the seed you thought had died comes back to life.

*A*s I was climbing out of the cave, I remember seeing a small green leaf that looked imprisoned in the stone. How could a little leaf breakthrough such deadness? The tomb was not a place of optimum conditions. No sunlight, little water, and yet the leaf still grew against all the odds.

Suddenly, as I was watching, the little leaf began to unfold, coming into existence. The leaf split open and broke apart due to its internal pressure. Each tenuous and delicate shoot pushed boldly, destroying the walls of its tomb. With green tints and varying shades of emerald, the leaf had been born! *Now is a time of new hope, leafiness, lushness, abundance*, I thought. The leaf was unrelenting, continuing without pause or interruption. Not yielding in strength or determination.

Looking at me, he said, "So much work had to be done underground."

I knew he was talking about the cave.

"On the surface, it looked like abandonment and loneliness, but at your darkest and blackest points, I poured hope and rain and possibilities into you. Anytime I lead you into the wilderness, it's for a divine purpose. Everything has something to reveal to you. You have to adjust your vision in the darkness."

Reflections

Leafiness, the bursting forth of the first sweet, tender leaves pushing through the soil after the long winter has passed is truly an inspiration. What I thought had died had come back to life.

During the winter, this lush leafiness is not apparent; the plant looks dead, yet with the return of spring, the leaf unrelentingly pushes through the obstacles.

I began to realize I can have new leafiness, even though I am sick.

On difficult days, my thoughts can push through the darkness just as a new leaf pushes through its night.

Even though my Crohn's disease doesn't let me eat so many of the foods I enjoy, my mind can feed itself on meals of wisdom, knowledge, and understanding.

God resurrects us from the dead, but we must go through it, not around it. We must go through the graveyard.

"Lord, what did you save my life for?"

"Because there is something you are supposed to do with it."

17

CHRISTMAS FIRE

Nothing is going to startle us more when we pass through the veil to the other side than to realize how well we know our Father and how familiar his face is to us.
—**Ezra Taft Benson**

*I*t was nearly Christmas. My house was decorated festively with old-fashioned charm and radiated a warm, cozy glow. The stately evergreen tree in the corner of my living room released the scent of pine through every nook and cranny of my home. It took me days and days to put up rope garland and twinkling lights, not to mention decorating the tree, but it was worth it!

I've loved the Christmas season ever since I was a small child, but once I became sick, many of the Christmas traditions (the sugar cookies, the baking, and candies) were now stored in my memory. Christmas Eve dawned as peacefully as I had imagined. My family was near, and plans for Christmas Eve were in progress. As the day wore on, I began to feel unrelenting pain in my lower abdomen. Crohn's was supposed to be on holiday over Christmas, wasn't it? I pushed on, preparing for our family Christmas Eve.

It was early evening when my family arrived. Hugs and happiness filled the air . . . until I was admitted to the hospital on Christmas Eve 2012 with another bowel obstruction. As usual, a nasogastric tube was inserted into my right nostril, extending down into my stomach. My fever rose, and my health was declining.

As I lay sad and restless in my hospital bed, sweet Christmas music played softly on the TV in my room. My heart was sick. Who wants to be in the hospital anytime, but especially on Christmas Eve?

As the evening advanced, a nurse came in to check my vitals. She mentioned that my blood pressure was a little high but reassured me it was probably from the high dose of prednisone I had resumed. However, later that evening all hell broke loose. Monitors and beepers were sounding the alarm that something was wrong. The charge nurse came bursting into my room, and supervisors were scrambling. My blood pressure was 220/140. It seemed as if all of the elements of my diseases simultaneously began an attack. I had dropped to a near-death state.

Death was around every corner. He never stayed long, just long enough to plant the thought of dying in my mind and then leave. Several urgent calls were made to my doctor regarding my situation. A new medication was prescribed, and eventually my blood pressure was within the normal range again.

My storms had been so mighty, my suffering so horrific. My soul longed to be free from satan's binding chains, from the threats of death. It was then my Creator and friend entered my room.

"I am here," he said, reaching for my hand.

Reflections

I was so disappointed lying in my hospital bed on Christmas Eve. How eagerly I had looked forward to being with my children and grandchild, playing games, eating (well, at least they could eat), and unwrapping presents. I had imagined how this evening would play out in my head countless times, but never once did I guess my being in the hospital would be part of my Christmas Eve.

I knew I would be spending several days in the hospital with a tube up my nose and vast amounts of meds entering my body.

The beautiful Christmas music, movies, and programming helped, and the nurses were empathic and kind. My family came up often to visit me, but I know they were as disappointed as I was.

18

FIRE ON THE MOUNTAIN

If God lights the fire, no devil in hell can stop it.

I was released shortly after New Years. I had missed Christmas. As I opened the door to my home, I saw my tree still standing in the corner. Later that night I sat down and looked at all the familiar decorations and twinkling Christmas lights. I sighed. As soon as my strength returned, I would need to get busy putting Christmas back in a box until next year.

"Come with me," he said softly.

We had taken a limited number of steps when we entered a wooded area graced with earthy smelling wetness. The sky was cloudy, the air damp as if from recent rain.

"The very thing satan built up around you will fuel you into your destiny. Your sickness will propel you into a greater purpose."

Scanning the landscape, I saw a forested area a short distance away. Countless timeworn trees, limbs, and branches revealed visible signs of past mighty storms. Dark green moss was emerging from the broken trees. Ferns with their feathery, leafy fronds covered the woodland floor. Before long, a weather-beaten wood structure appeared in front of us. Long, green ivy vines entangled themselves around the dilapidated shed.

"Ivy vines won't easily let go of something they are attached to," he pointed out. "These vines are resistant to pulling and breaking. The ivy plant is also a strong plant that can grow in the hardest environment. Those vines remind me of you," he said, looking over at me. "All tangled up."

Then he added, "Just like those vines are intertwined, you and I are woven together. It's not so much of what I reveal to you, my child, as the linking up of your frail nature with my limitless divine powers. I'm not on the other side of the curtain, waiting to see how you handle things. The whole time I'm whispering in your ear that I'm right here with you."

His words sank into my heart with a power that caught me off guard. I would discover the authority of those words soon enough.

"Everything in my kingdom world is counterintuitive."

"Go on," I said.

"You are richer when you go through trials. When you try to avoid your trials, your life is actually diminished."

"I have it all backward, don't I?" I grinned sheepishly.

He smiled back at me.

I was captivated by his commonness, yet I knew there was nothing commonplace about him. I noticed back behind the shed were acres of trees densely packed together. These thick coniferous forests consisted primarily of the lodgepole pine. Reaching for my hand, we began walking in the direction of the woods. As we hiked further into the woodlands, the landscape became drier and drier. Bugs zipped in and out of my ears, humming and buzzing their little songs. Prickly moss began to emerge from the fractured logs. Before long, dried brown ferns soon covered the woodland floor. The dense shoulder-high thickets were almost impossible to walk through.

As we continued through the forest, I grasped the scent of something: smoke.

I scanned ahead and stared as the horizon grew orange. The trees were on fire. Mountains, prominent cliffs, thousands of trees, and boulders came into view as I absorbed my surroundings. A wildfire was blazing fiercely. The dry timber must have flared up at the touch of a match or perhaps a lightning strike. The fire was uncontrolled, very intense, and spreading rapidly. I could hear the crackling of the fire and trees crashing. The trees looked like smoldering wicks.

I wanted to run but didn't know which way to go. For an instant I recalled running away at the lake when the death angel had appeared. He had told me to stay near him so I wouldn't need to run. Yet somehow, in the smoke and haze, I could not find him. I panicked. I found myself standing on the edge of an expansive abyss that plummeted and plunged into deepness. I could not endure the searing heat; the fumes were choking. The depths churned like a boiling caldron, just as the blood inside me had boiled when my fever skyrocketed.

A large mass of smoke billowed up the vast cavern. I wondered how much of me would be left if I made it out of hell. Glancing down, I caught sight of my hands. Both hands were covered with scratches and cuts. Calluses and blisters uttered the cry of feet that had been on a grueling journey. I remembered the words he had spoken to me just hours before:

"I'm right here, whispering in your ear. I'm right here with you."

The flames blazed in a frenzy. A blast of heat nearly overcame me. I could not go back; the flames had trapped me. I forced my way, pulling and straining to get ahead of the fire. Broken, jagged bolts of lightning moved in closer the higher I climbed. The rarified atmosphere oppressed my breathing. I was exhausted and confused; fear held me tightly. I was afraid he would abandon me. My heart was pounding and my legs quivered. It was then I saw a sign of activity. I was apprehensive about moving forward because I could not see through the wall of flames. Squinting my eyes, I saw the Creator walking toward me. Collapsing with relief, I fell into his arms.

"I am right here with you. I am beside you. I understand all your weaknesses and see your struggles. Imagine the invisible forces all working on your behalf under my direction. Keep them in mind. You will feel stronger. I am a strategic God. You are right where you are supposed to be to align you with your purpose."

With my hand in his, we climbed higher. Far off in the distance, I noticed a cave dug into a hillside. The cave was almost indistinguishable through the smoke, yet it was there.

After all we had been through together, I knew he only had what was best for me in his heart. I lifted my eyes to look into his face. He had not left me. He would never leave me. He stood next to me, gently squeezing my hand, just as he had held my hand through every part of my journey. I felt very frail and nearly extinguished. There was nothing left of me. I thought back to the first time He had asked for my hand and how thankful I was that I had placed my hand in His.

"Your destiny is very near," he said, looking down at me. "The enemy fights so hard not because of what you have done, but what you are going to do. Attacks increase to defeat you."

When we arrived at this cavity in the mountain, calmness occupied the empty space. A sweet fragrance surrounded us. Surprisingly, it was not the smell of death but the fragrance of life.

My thoughts rambled as I recalled my long journey, my diagnosis of Crohn's disease, rheumatoid arthritis, and lupus. My resistance to surrendering my old self.

The battles I fought when leaving my old life, the storms, the endless hospital stays. The mighty blows of loss, grief and abandonment I endured. I learned to live rejected, humiliated, isolated, frightened and full of doubt. I have gone into combat with pain and suffering and the struggles of uncertainty that wore away my faith.

"My gift to you comes with your surrender to my plan for you. It is then the power of my gift is released."

"You are now filled with meaning and purpose. After experiencing all you have gone through, you have your story to share with others. You had to learn more to be more. You had to experience humiliation to understand how it feels. You were the field, the seed. You needed to be plowed, broken open. You were dug into the rawness of the soil and prepared to live in the blackness under the earth. Eventually you pushed through, even though you could not see a thing. So much work had to be done underground. On the surface it looked like abandonment and loneliness, but at your darkest and blackest points, I poured hope and rain and possibilities into you. Everything has something to reveal to you."

I was so exhausted. I moved toward a flat rock inside the cave, laid myself down on it, and closed my eyes. He was holding my hand. I knew he would never leave me, never. I heard him speak words from Ezekiel 37:4 to me: "I will make breath enter you, and you will come to life."

I do not know if all of my vital functions and processes shut down as in actual death, but I do know this: I died. I don't mean I died physically, although I had been near physical death many times. I died to my will, to myself. This death was about obedience and love. Why would someone make such a sacrifice or, more accurately, be willing to become the sacrifice? There is only one reason so strong, so powerful, so passionate as to have that kind of effect. It must be love. Death seems like the end, but it is really the beginning.

Before I knew it, we were far from the cave and the wildfire. We walked silently, hand in hand, as we headed back toward the dilapidated shed. I looked for the ivy growing on the shed and was stunned to discover the fire had burned everything to a crisp. Each step of the blackened ground raised clouds of dust and ash.

One cannot discover a nugget in the ashes without realizing the price. I looked around; this fire had left scars. How do you take the fire of adversity and glean the nuggets of wisdom from the ashes? The nuggets of wisdom and learning have gone through the fire. Nuggets of wisdom are learned by walking the path. There are spiritual gems to be recovered from severe changes.

But just as one carelessly left spark can ignite a firestorm, leaving death and utter destruction in its wake, that is not the end. It looks like the end; it feels like the end; it even smells of death. And for a while, death is all around you. Somewhere under the blackened earth and heavy ashes, though, the ground is stirring. The ashes now say to the soil, "It is time for the miracle of the seed!" For out of the ashes, I was being prepared for a new life.

Reflections

I used to think my sickness robbed me of who I was. I now know my sickness made me who I am.

I think of the inflammation that continues to try and destroy me. My immune system is overly active and cannot tell the difference between healthy cells and unhealthy cells and would continue to kill me if it were not for the immunosuppressant medication I receive.

Just as the tangled ivy was demolished by fire, the fire in my body is still trying to demolish me. Yet I have learned that through adversity there are nuggets in the ashes.

19

THE FIRE OF REBIRTH

You must do the thing you think you cannot do.
—Eleanor Roosevelt

To my delight, we returned to the lake where we had spent so many hours together. We sat down, just as we had done countless times before. The small, gentle waves were rolling up on the shore, and the warm sand climbed in between my toes.

Looking over at me, he smiled. "You are now connected to something bigger than yourself. You are now acquainted with shame. I am asking you to go into shame and bring hope. To go into darkness and bring light. To go into sadness and bring love."

I closed my eyes and let his words wash over me. They were both challenging and exciting.

"Even before you faced your diseases, you asked me to broaden the scope of your mind so that you could begin to see how to help others. I took your small telescope and gave you a broader capacity so you can begin to see what I see. Look beyond your small circle. Allow yourself to dream once more."

Looking out over the lake, he rose and walked toward the water. With every step, the water rose higher and higher on him. He turned to look at me and motioned for me to join him. Instantly, I remembered our first meeting at the lake when he had walked into the water, just as he was doing now. I recalled how the water had reached my neck, knowing that one more step toward him would cause the water to rise over my head.

I didn't hesitate this time.

As I walked into the deep toward him, his tender words came to mind: "Surrender is a choice of the heart." Since the first time I heard them, they have become like priceless gems.

Reflections

Most days, I recognize that I am not as powerless as I used to feel. I know that I am not that person anymore who felt useless and inferior. At least most days, I know that.

I continually struggle with the realities of Crohn's disease, lupus, and rheumatoid arthritis. I still experience days when doubt and despair are nearby.

Every time I put my socks and shoes on is a victory. Every time I walk through the grocery store is a victory. Every time I get an injection is a victory. Every time I enjoy the trees and birds at my bird feeders, the sky and clouds, or search for joy on the dreary days is a victory. And on days when there is no victory to be found, and there are days like that, I give myself permission to be at peace with my situation.

Epilogue

There are many things I can't explain. I learned to recognize that I was being tenderly prepared for something I could not have done as my old self. At the lake, sometimes there were no profound words exchanged or new revelations revealed; we just sat there, side by side, sometimes in the daylight and sometimes at night, with beams of moonlight reflecting across the lake. Those times with him brought great peace and comfort to my soul when everything in my natural world was chaos. He helped me see with fresh eyes and a new perspective.

Are my attitudes broader, my views more tolerant, my beliefs healthier, and my faith growing? Yes, I have grown, just like the little leaf that pushed through the hardships in the cave, reaching for the light.

As I continue on my journey, there is one thing I know now for sure. The Creator is love—refreshing and life-giving love. And a single drop of his love creates life.

Scientists and researchers the world over will never be able to create, replicate, or duplicate living life-giving properties of one drop of his love. One drop, even a tiny droplet, evokes hope. Power is activated, and life itself begins to stir. One drop of love to a broken person or child makes you a life-giver, just like resurrection himself.

He offers us all droplets of love.

> *Of one thing I am perfectly sure;*
> *God's story never ends with ashes.*
> **—Elizabeth Elliott**

About the Author

SANDRA SIEMENS is a licensed independent social worker with over twenty years in the counseling field. She founded her own Christian counseling corporation in 2000 and has been a popular speaker at numerous Christian women's conferences, quickly building rapport through sharing her story, humor, and enthusiasm.

She is a member of the PHI ALPHA National Social Work Honor Society and a charter member of the American Association of Christian Counselors. Sandy now resides in Cheyenne, Wyoming.

You can learn more about Sandy at:

www.sandrasiemens.com

9 781947 360686